# ROME

## IMPRESSIONS, RECOLLECTIONS AND CHARM

**WHITE STAR**

P U B L I S H E R S

# ROME
## IMPRESSIONS, RECOLLECTIONS AND CHARM

*Written by*
Laura Delli Colli

*Photographs*
Cesare Gerolimetto

*Editorial director*
Valeria Manferto De Fabianis

*Art director and drawings*
Patrizia Balocco Lovisetti

*Translation*
Antony Shugaar

The author wishes to thank Chiara Fasanelli for her valuable assistance.

*Page 1*
The Pantheon Fountain (1575), Piazza della Rotonda.

*Pages 2-3*
Trevi Fountain (1732-1763).

*Pages 4-5*
The Fontana dei Fiumi, or Fountain of the Four Rivers, (1650-1651), Piazza Navona.

*Pages 6-7*
Via Conciliazione and St. Peter's Basilica (1506-1614).

*Page 8*
Ponte (Bridge) Vittorio Emanuele II with Gianicolo (Janiculum) Hill in the background.

*Page 9*
Statue of the Angel with the Crown of Thorns (1667-1669), Ponte Sant'Angelo.

*Pages 10-11*
The Colosseum (72-82 A.D.).

*Pages 12-13*
Castel Sant'Angelo (140 A.D.) was rebuilt in the sixteenth century.

© 1995, 1999 White Star S.r.l.
Via Candido Sassone, 22/24
13100 Vercelli, Italy
www.whitestar.it

ISBN 88-8095-343-5

Reprints:

  3 4 5 6   06 05 04 03 02

Printed in Italy

IN·AERVMNA·MEA
DVM·CONFIGITVR·SPINA

# INTRODUCTION

Eternal Rome. Sacred Rome. Secular Rome. Aristocratic and arrogant, ancient and modern, rhetorical and opulent and yet minimalist, Rome is the city of little things, of hidden corners, of breathtaking colors in a chanced upon dawn or blood red sunset. It is hard to find words that will not seem exaggerated. The best way is to look through the cold eyes of the reporter, and undoubtedly, through those of History. Mysterious and inscrutable, Rome is a truly unique city. It has inspired poets, painters, and great artists of all times. It has always been an obligatory point of passage in the evolution of numerous cultures, yet it has lost none of its spontaneity. Its inhabitants are sociable as nowhere else and will reserve a warm welcome for all, right down to the last of the occasional tourists.

Those visiting once, those passing through, and even those arriving on vacation all know from the very first that they will return. Rome is not easily forgotten. You will know it by its colors, its smells, its noises, even blindfolded. The perpetual charm prevails over the chaos, the smog, the disorganization, the noise, and the construction frauds that have fuelled controversy and discontent over the Rome of the twenty-first century. Unequalled anywhere in the world for its works of art, it is, first and foremost, ancient Rome. The sense of majesty in its monuments struck the great artist Giorgio De Chirico profoundly. After a brief period of study in the capital, he wrote that "In Rome the sense of prophecy is more extensive. A sensation of infinite and distant greatness. The same as that impressed by the Roman mason upon the

*Top*
A sweeping view of the Aventine Hill.

*Top*
Piazza del Campidoglio (sixteenth century).

*Right*
One of the dioscuri, Piazza del Campidoglio
(first century B.C.-third century A.D.).

arch, the reflection of that awe of the infinite which the celestial stratum sometimes produces in man." From white marble it has drawn the mark of immortality. The Mamertine prison, the ancient Cloaca Massima, and the Servian walls, which from the mid fourth century B.C. marked the confines of the city and saved it from Hannibal's horde, have all stood the test of time. The golden quadrangle of archaeology, a mine of information for researchers of all times, is still there circumscribed by the Palatine, Campidoglio, Viminal, and Quirinal despite the the asphalt strip called Via dei Fori Imperiali imposed by Mussolini during the years of fascism which cut the quadrangle in two. Inside the Roman Forum, the heart of the Roman Republic, are the remains of the ancient Curia, the Arch of Septimus Severus, the ruins of the temples of Saturn and the statues of the dioscuri, the temple of Antonino and Faustina, the House of the Vestal Virgins

and, lastly, the splendid Arch of Titus. The Imperial Forum complex contains the Colosseum and the remains of Trajan's Markets and Column.

The eye is lost in a maze of marble, here and there concealed by tufts of nettles. Wily cats, the true masters of ancient Rome, doze in opulence amid the House of Livia, the Domus Augustana, and the Thermae. The Palatine is considered the lap of Rome: in the times of the Emperors it was the heart of the city. On the Capitoline hill stood the temple of Jupiter, a fragment of ancient memories gone for ever. These re-emerge in the fourteenth century image of Petrarch crowned as a poet, or in the perfect geometrical lines of Michelangelo, who redesigned the Piazza del Campidoglio, initialing the paving. Passing today on those ancient stones are the Mayor and the Aldermen, as well as newly-wed couples for whom a photo with the Campidoglio as a backdrop or

beside the long stairway of Ara Coeli is a must. Even Bill and Hillary – Clinton, of course - posed amid the ancient Capitoline ruins during their celebrated Italian holiday, she smiling, dressed in fiery red, and he moved by the memories and charm of the ancient setting.

In the sixteenth century Rome enjoyed its second youth with the arrival of Bramante, Bernini, Borromini, Michelangelo, and Raphael. After centuries of darkness, the city began to put on a fresh face as new structures such as Palazzo Farnese, the Quirinal, Villa Medici, and Porta Pia by Michelangelo were erected as well as churches, the sacred soul of Rome.

This soul was also bound to tradition and culture through opera with that famous encounter in Sant'Andrea della Valle between Tosca and Cavaradossi. While sighs and murmurs seem to echo among the marble of the ancient church, the opera becomes life, reawakened by the aromas of the nearby restaurants, their names still celebrating Puccini's heroine in this city looking towards the third millenium. Sacred Rome offers the churches, the Pope and St Peter's Basilica with its Cupola, the Basilica of Santa Maria degli Angeli and that of St.s Peter and Paul. Sights and sensations include the smell of incense, floors polished by invisible attendants, and the passing of nimble altar boys. The ray of light piercing St Peter's from on high, like the withering eye of God, brings no feelings of fear. Those looking up towards the smallest ring of the dome are more likely to be dazzled. The imagination will race back in time to the

works planned by Bramante and carried out by Giuliano da Sangallo, then Raphael, Peruzzi, Sangallo again and, lastly, by Michelangelo with his special touch. There is the Dome, the colonnade, the Loggia, Raphael's rooms, and the final triumph of the Sistine Chapel. Oddly enough, it took the Japanese and their sponsorship to lift the haze of ancient patina and return the colors to their splendor as created by Michelangelo. However, this is part of the good and the bad of Rome: it is the home of the Romans but its offspring are citizens of the world.

Once upon a time for the populace of sacred and papal Rome the great Basilica was but a place of worship. It was not the city of the Pope but the burial place of Peter, founder of the Catholic Church. The Borgo district soon took on an international air. Representing the heart and soul of St Peter's, its name comes from the German burg, a German matrix for a mesh of streets and alleys untouched by time and, in some corners, by light too. The Borgo streets are part of the appeal and heart of

*Left*
Interior of the Basilica di San Paolo fuori le Mura (fourth-ninth centuries A.D.). Saint Paul Outside the Walls was rebuilt in 1854.

*Top*
The statue of Rome (1471), Piazza del Campidoglio.

*Top*
The statue of the Angel with the Lance
and Castel Sant'Angelo.

*Right*
Detail of Ponte Sant'Angelo, or Sant'Angelo
Bridge, (second century A.D.) with the castle in
the background.

papal Rome. Passing through them today one is unaware of all the history in these narrow little streets. Today the shop windows glitter with holy souvenirs. Miniatures of the Basilica are flanked by portable replicas of the Pietà, glass domes contain the Cupola in a snow storm, and t-shirts bear the Pope's image. To think that in the times of Boniface VIII and the great invention of the Jubilee, Borgo was the Christian soul of the city and the expression of the impervious road to Heaven, symbolized at the end of the darkness by the shaft of light and the silhouette of the great dome.

With St. Peter's as Heaven, Peter's tomb represents the highest and mightiest symbol of the city of God. Built up haphazardly and then hewn down by the urban renewal which destroyed it, the Borgo district has nonetheless maintained its "color." Small shops line narrow streets where the buildings huddle together, including the barber shop, the

old cobbler, the tailor, the bakery with the fragrant smell of bread cooked in a wood oven, the pizza place with its old sign, the old grocery stores, and the chair-weavers. Strangely enough, all this has just as much to do with holy Rome as the black habits dotting the white square which conjure up the seventeenth century's black costumes and wall hangings, representing the color of mourning and the Inquisition. Two dates reawaken in the Romans the mysteries and secrets of the temporal power of the Church. On September 11, 1599, Beatrice Cenci, victim of a family tragedy now a legend in Rome, was punished, and on February 17, 1600, Giordano Bruno was burned at the stake. Today, Monte Cenci smells of traditional Roman fritti and carciofi alla giudìa, while in Piazza Farnese, shoppers at the oldest and most popular market of the city jostle around the block commemorating Giordano Bruno.

Secular Rome can be found in the villas, gardens, and the carnival celebrations in baroque Piazza Navona. Further back in history, gladiators fought in the Colosseum and blood ran over the travertine of the Flavian Amphitheater as the fighters of Ancient Rome entered the arena to amuse the Emperor. Chosen from among prisoners of war, criminals, slaves, and volunteers, they were destined to die and fought for the delight of the public. Only the mercy or a whim of the Emperor could save their lives. Secular Rome could also be cruel at times.

There was the crazy Rome of Nero's follies and the magnificent Rome of the baroque Carnevale, with Piazza Navona flooded to become a pool. Rome has its records and history, its curiosities and legends such as the time when at the end of the seventeenth century a poetry presentation on the Campidoglio sought the enchantment of Olympia. For the Arcadian poets Rome was to be the new paradise, an Olympus of secularity and poetry under the banner of Pan and his pipes. The Campidoglio was transformed into a bucolic rendez-vous and the poets sought new life in the breath of secular Rome. Thinking back, the atmosphere must have been like that of an ephemeral Roman summer ante litteram with free verse in the spirit of the pastoral world. Shepherds and inspiring nymphs would be found where Roman senators had stood, while Greek-style tunics would have fluttered in the place of the purple-edged laticlavium of the Imperial senators. A truly profane rejoicing, the Arcadia marked its days with hedonistic love affairs. However, intermediary love poems and literary mediocrity soon lost momentum.

*Right*
The Obelisk of Santa Maria sopra Minerva, Piazza della Minerva (sixth century A.D.).

*Pages 24-25*
The Steps of Trinità dei Monti (1724-1726).

*Top*
Piazza Navona.

Passing through Rome, Carlo Goldoni, with a hint of superiority, branded the ancien regime culture of Arcadia in his Memoires, caustically ridiculing Sybil and the oracles decorated with drooping laurel..

The romantic strolls of the poets on their cultural travels were characteristic of secular Rome. Keats, Byron, and Shelley, along with Stendhal's "Les Promenades dans Rome," Goethe's "Italian Journey," and the secret, scandalous itineraries of Roger Peyrefitte were followed by contemporary writers such as Truman Capote, Gore Vidal. One place that conjures up the artists and Bohemia of this aspect of Rome is the ancient Cafè Greco, just one step away from Piazza di Spagna, two from the stairway, three from Via del Corso, and four from Via del Babuino.

Now, the cups with the gold and bright orange stripe are sold as souvenirs, but the worn marble tables and the slightly misshapen floor reveal more sumptuous times. No mention is made of forbidden love affairs, surreptitious encounters, passionate betrayals, and agonizing platonic loves. Oscar Wilde came often to Italy. He lived in Rome and extolled it after his stay in 1877. His verses, inspired by Shelley, Byron, and Keats, who had all preceded him in the Italian pilgrimage, perfectly convey the romanticism and pagan glorification of the Rome fantasized about by the English poets. The author of Salome wrote odes to the tombs of Shelley and Keats. Reading those verses, the profane grandeur of this romantic city sends the imagination racing to that red house on Piazza di Spagna where the poet lived, and to the colors, the noises,

the creaking of the last carriages on the stones of Piazza di Spagna, and the wan light of the sunset when the stairway lit up with stars, as opposed to the neon signs now coldly indicating the entrance to fast food eating places, or the underground which every fifteen minutes from beneath the steps of Trinità dei Monti vomits hordes of tourists, more interested in a pair of jeans than in lost sentiment. The poetry of that unique staircase will not, nonetheless, die. It will endure the crowds of springtime tourists which turn the travertine streets worn by centuries of passing feet into an anthill of upturned heads, all gazing at Villa Medici. It will likewise endure the onset of summer, when it becomes a catwalk . in honor of high fashion as Valentino and Armani sit in the front row and, together with the stars of international show business, applaud Claudia Schiffer and Naomi Campbell. On that night the splendor of the stairway disappears as if by magic and the fascination of Piazza di Spagna fades in the evanescent light of a luxury fashion show.

Yet, when the spotlights go off, Trinità dei Monti becomes itself again, the intense pink and bright red of its azaleas like fireworks lighting up the white travertine. Meanwhile, the guitars and flutes of the odd eccentric tourist will accompany his search for lost coins here and there amid the fluttering ribbon of people climbing and descending to the silver blade of Via Condotti, historically the most fashionable street facing the steps.

This is the heart of luxury shopping and "Made in Italy" style, where the wealthiest tourists are attracted by designer labels such as Bulgari, Giorgio Armani, Prada, Ferragamo, and Battistoni.

The words of the poet Alfonso Gatto say much about the atmosphere of secular Rome between the two wars: "I had just arrived in Rome from Salerno and I was still dazed. My poet friend, older than I, said, 'This evening I'll show you the king of Rome.' 'Who is it?' 'Scipione!' We went all over. To Aragno's, Piazza del Popolo, Piazza Navona. Nothing. Not a trace of this Scipione. It was almost daylight and we were about to return home, cold and disappointed, when on Gianicolo Hill we saw a bonfire and a crowd of people shouting excitedly. There were half-dressed whores and, at the center, there he was making obscene gestures illuminated by the firelight. I, who had come from Salerno, asked my friend 'Where have you brought me?.'"

Scipione is one of few contemporary artists to have grasped the intoxification of "pagan" Rome. He is especially sensitive to its colors like the reddish glare of some of the façades in Piazza Navona and the blinding white of the statues which seems to bring them to life, making them speak and palpitate.

Rome can also be arrogant with its noble palaces and the power that lurks in Montecitorio or the Vatican.

*Left, top*
The courtyard of San Silvestro
(eighth century A.D.).

*Left, bottom*
Piazza dei Mercanti, Trastevere.

*Top*
The Arco degli Acetati, between Pellegrino
Street and Campo de' Fiori.

29

Federico Fellini lived a stone's throw from Piazza del Popolo, and his home became a rendez-vous for the film world, politicians, journalists, and high society. He understood this aspect of Rome so well that he presented it with the most cruelly honest portraits of its shortcomings in Roma, Satyricon, and La Dolce Vita. In 1960, while the intelligentsia was meeting at the fashionable Café de Paris and Doney's, Via Veneto was the fulcrum of high society life. Here were the friends of Pannunzio's Il Mondo, as well as any film stars passing through. Rome was becoming a philosophy, a way of life, no longer a mere city. Bustling away, Rome became a great setting for the artists who immortalized its suburbs, substance, color, lifestyle, and its very spirit. It was transformed into a set destined to make a permanent mark on the history of Italian theatre, as well as that of the great Hollywood film world. The fairy tale of "Hollywood on the Tiber" was born as paparazzi, high society, and vacant cocktail parties catered to the public relations of the stars. In Via Veneto a famous restaurant where Richard Burton wooed Liz Taylor still conserves mementoes of their passage through Rome. Gossip and scandals soon followed. The city was the backdrop and its Sixties were colored with romance.

Rome's arrogance, cinematographical in this case, snowballed. Great actors, great films, great investments in celluloid, and legendary grandeur in the studios welcomed for the first time the smell of greenbacks and the great names from Los Angeles.

Luxury restaurants and glittering hotels were the stage for the caprices of the stars. Fellini and Flaiano did not invent a character like Marcello in "La Dolce Vita" by chance. That fashionable and vain segment of the Rome that had won over the hearts of foreigners, and of Hollywood, really existed. It was an ongoing exhibition of vanity, grown out of the ruins of neo-realistic Rome as immortalized by Roberto Rossellini. The rhythm really was like that of the transient cardboard set. As 1959 was coming to a close and "La Dolce Vita" was about to launch Via Veneto as a must for wealthy high society the world over, Flaiano, speaking about the atmosphere in Rome the morning after the follies and caprices of the nocturnal jet set, said, "the air was clear then, the traffic quiet, and from the baker's shop wafted the smell of hot croissants. There was a jolly, small town bustle, journalists and writers were having a drink before lunch, the painters had no dealers, and people did not take planes much...."

Today Via Veneto is regular location for events. Every film or society occasion is an excuse to rekindle memories or tune in to the waves of revival. Doney's, the Café de Paris, and Harry's Bar have resisted. Unfortunately, the old bakery smelling of fresh bread has been suffocated

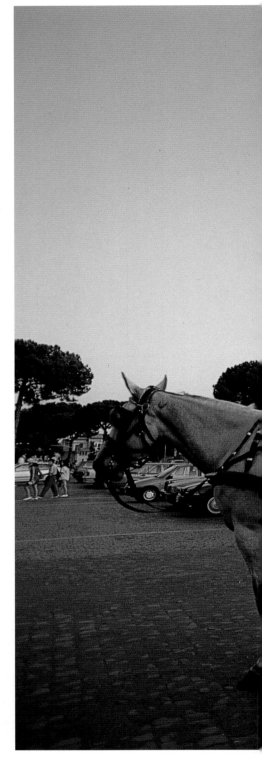

*Top*
Altare della Patria (1885-1911).

by banks. The ritual of the intellectual aperitif has faded with time, lost in the rapid consumption of a quick sandwich or the business brunch of the street's new inhabitants. Those white collars with their gray jackets and regimental ties regularly step out with their mobile phones in their pockets, ready to fly off.

It is difficult, or rather impossible, to restore the Via Veneto of the past and to bring "La Dolce Vita" back to life thirty years later. Valentino, fashion designer par excellence and dressmaker to the great ladies of the world, tried for fun to revive the splendid image of "La Dolce Vita" of the past by bringing a new Anita Ekberg to Trevi Fountain. But can a Claudia Schiffer embody the charm and opulence of Fellini's star of the Sixties? In Rome, the magic of that period was nearly rediscovered for one night.

Rome is a rhetorical, aulic, and imposing city with great palaces where the strategies of power are decided. It is a city of ritual appointments. One is the Pope's Angelus every Sunday at noon in Piazza San Pietro. There is always a crowd of applauding believers, although in recent years there has also been a host of rolling TV cameras carrying the Pope's message and blessing to the whole universe of followers tuned in at home. The square starts to fill from the early hours of the morning with hordes of tourists and buses filled with chattering pilgrims from near and far. A multicolored mass of appreciative men and women raise their eyes to the Pope's window asking for a glance, a word, or just a nod of the head. Another rapt and applauding crowd can be found at the Quirinal for the changing of the guard.

*Top*
The Temple of Vesta (second century B.C.), Piazza Bocca della Verità.

*Right*
The Temple of Aesculapius (eighteenth century A.D.), Villa Borghese gardens.

*Top*
Fontana dei Fiumi (1650-1651),
Piazza Navona.

*Pages 36-37*
A carriage in St Peter's Square.

On the other hand, there is the annual rhetoric of the Roman Christmas, a street festival which continues to offer its lights and colorful markets selling cheap dreams in baroque Piazza Navona. While the consumer rites of shoppers are celebrated in the golden streets of the old city center, the lights of Piazza Navona come on in anticipation of the Epiphany. For the Romans, Piazza Navona is the home of the friendly old hag of the Epiphany and where one can, now at great expense, purchase gifts for the traditional stocking as well as the latest handmade Nativity scenes made by craftsmen from Naples with little statues made of the traditional papier-mâché and colored chalk of the Christmas mangers of yesteryear in defiance of today's plastic ones.

Rhetorical Rome preserves its traditions. On Sunday mornings in the Pincio gardens with the swans' on the lake, the pony and cart await smiling children.

On Gianicolo (Janiculum) Hill, Rome still renders homage to Garibaldi, but the midday canon blast is now deadened by horns and droning engines. Only in the Pincio gardens of Rome, every Sunday morning, the puppet show is repeated for the youngest spectators. Punch has had the same voice for forty, perhaps fifty, years. It is now recorded and transmitted to preserve the charm, but once upon a time the slightly nasal tones were heard live every week as the live applause of the small crowd of onlookers greeted their hero.

Rome is also the city of mothers and children, and of wives and girlfriends. It is famous for stolen kisses before the loveliest panorama of the city, sighs captured among the stately busts in the Pincio gardens, or slightly over-audacious caresses in the dark while descending from the great terrace to Villa Medici and then further down to the stairway of Piazza di Spagna.

In the times of Shelley and Keats, rhetorical Rome was heard in the sound of a carriage on the cobbles. More recently, it was the guitar of some hippy passing through or a crackling pan of chestnuts at the foot of the Spanish steps. Yesterday the chestnut sellers were Romans, their cheeks burned by the first of the north winds. Today, at even the most inconvenient hours, the grills are subcontracted out, perhaps to some north African who has already learnt all he needs to know from the dying breed of chestnut-sellers, such as how to make more money by not completely filling the shriveled paper cone.

Minimalist Rome is also an everyday city. It is anything but the city of legend and courtly poems.

Contemporary Rome consists of real life, everyday noises, mopeds darting away at green lights, road sweepers in action, and restaurants smelling of spring lamb and meatballs, ribbon pasta and fried dishes, spaghetti with tomato and basil sauce with a mountain of Parmesan cheese sprinkled over it, and meat as red as the sunsets over the Pincio hill. The noise of the traffic fails to totally cover the sounds of the traditional crafts. It seems incredible but on some days, in some places and streets, the musical lament of the knife-grinder seeking knives to sharpen and the refrain of the umbrella-mender who changes the ribs of broken umbrellas still rise above the din of engines and televisions. TV aerials tower above ancient palaces, satellite dishes appear on the terraces of the "better" districts, but the voice of the old craftsmen can still be heard. It is not an issue if the knife-grinder now uses a motor instead of bicycle pedals to turn his stone, or if the umbrella-mender uses better tools than in times gone by.

The Rome of today, with a few too many fast food restaurants and large suburban stores, is living on interest from its past, cultivating its own philosophy of life. In art, this minimalist, commonplace Rome harks back to Mafai's taverns, Vittorio De Sica's neo-realistic bicycles, the visionary and sanguinary city of Scipione, the ideal Rome of Siron, and to the black and white Rome of Pasolini's decadence in the films Mamma Roma and Accattone.

Rome is a city of fiery moods and strong tones, of unique color and magic light. Famous photographers and leading film directors are well aware of the importance of catching a color, a frame, or an image of Rome at the right moment. Rome will awaken and suddenly come alive as the hearts of its statues seem to revive. The sun turns the contours of the dioscuri pink, then golden, blood red, and brown. The night sky silhouettes the unmistakable outline of the Colosseum and illuminates the whiteness of the Pincio with pale moonlight. One and only Rome is proud and sensual, a little haughty in the sunlight, silvery and pale when the moon comes out, veiled with mist when the southeast wind delays the rising sun, and somber and gray when the sky unexpectedly clouds over and rain pours menacingly on the ancient marbles and baroque lines of the great statues. The magic moment is at sunset, when the red houses light up with tones as warm as the burning sun. This is the hour of the artists, poets, and photographers, when the last boatmen plough across the tawny Tiber River. For visitors, it is an enchanting moment that generates sensations and feelings unique to Rome.

*Top and pages 40-41*
At Cinecittà, the plaster statue storeroom.

*Everything lights up only to dim in the Roman twilight before the night comes alive. At this point in the day, Rome shows its other face, black as ink but alive with inimitable fragrances such as the mint growing wild amid the ruins of the Forum, or the perfume of the last oranges left battling against the concrete on the Aventine Hill. The citrus trees may be a little wild but they are as ancient as the gardens they belong to, from where they gaze beyond the Tiber to where the minimalist Rome of the last surviving craftsmen and that somewhat exaggeratedly folkloristic neighborhood Trastevere (made so for foreign tourists) indulge in the last, daily rituals of the popular and wily city which grew up in the shadow of the Pope-King.*

*Bottom*
The sacred area (third-first centuries B.C.), Largo di Torre Argentina.

*Right*
The Temple of Apollo Sosiano (fourth-first century B.C.). The Synagogue (1904) can be seen in the background.

*Pages 44-45*
The Imperial Forum (second-first centuries B.C.).

*Pages 46-47*
Statues on Ponte Vittorio Emanuele II, with the dome of St. Peter's in the background.

*Pages 48-49*
Details of statues in the Fontana dei
Fiumi (1650-1651), Piazza Navona

# A STUNNING BEAUTY

"Without having seen Rome one cannot rightly imagine the effect it can have. It seems a city observed through a glass which magnifies its contours. One would say that the houses, the squares, the churches, the fountains, the steps, the columns, and all the monuments in Rome were created by a race of men physically twice our size. One must crane one's neck to see the tops of the buildings and columns. One needs a telescope to see the end of the squares and a carriage to move about. As a city it is astounding — that is the right word. The first instinct felt is the need to have someone alongside and to clutch his arm so tight as to bruise him. Were it not for the people all around one would cry out."

Edmondo De Amicis,
"Ricordi di Roma," from
Ricordi del 1870-1871,
Florence: Barbera, 1873.

## *"J'AI PLUS DE SOUVENIR QUE SI J'AVAIS MILLE ANS"*

*"To speak of Rome is for me a sweet but serious task. Sweet because no subject attracts me or gratifies me more. Serious not just because Rome is Rome, but rather because I have lived in this city for more than a quarter of a century and I could use Baudelaire's words to say of it, 'J'ai plus de souvenirs que si j'avais mille ans.' I have seen the waiters of the Cafè Aragno grow old, the women I have loved or liked in youth fade, many illusions and many friendships go to ruin, but Rome has been transformed, rejuvenated, and has grown year by year, with no mercy for our personal attachments and melancholies. Oh no, Rome is no easy city, no kind city!"*

Vincenzo Cardarelli,
Cielo sulle Città,
Milan: Bompiani, 1939.

*Top*
Columns of the Temple of Apollo Sosiano
(fourth-first centuries B.C.). In the
background, the Teatro Marcello (first
century B.C. - fourth century A.D.).

*Right*
The Arch of Septimus Severus
(second century A.D.), Roman Forum.

# TO ROME, THE ETERNAL CITY

"Eternal spirit, eternal courage, oh Rome! After all the blood, after a long period of oblivion, the raging thunder and the feeble silence, so many downfalls and so many flames lit by all the winds, you with your own feet treading on your ashes, your ruins ever higher, you celebrate the greatest of your triumphs, that you have beaten death. You before all the peoples that you called to be rightly yours, now you appear again in the first flower of youth, extraordinary, like Pallante, defended all around by glittering weapons and with the sword; and hanging above the world that light with which lit the peoples all their light, that which breaks our obscurity. Oh mighty Rome, the mighty yours more than time the lamp of life."

Giovanni Pascoli,
Poemi del Risorgimento,
Bologna: Zanichelli, 1913.

*Left*
Detail of Trajan's Column
(first century A.D.).

*Top*
Detail of the Arch of Septimus Severus
(second century A.D.).

*Pages 54-55*
The Forum of Trajan (first century A.D.).

# A GLANCE, AN EMBRACE...

*"Looking down, from the roof of the church to where you have just been, you will see a procession of ants. You can only just make out the people strolling in the square, the two large fountains seem two quivering white plumes, and the smaller domes of the Basilica those little bells used for the statues of saints. All the city is embraced at a glance. The first thing you notice are the walls of the Colosseum and the Thermae, huge and black. The statues on the top of the columns, the tips of the obelisks, the curving banks of the Tiber, Pincio hill, Villa Borghese, the Quirinal, San Giovanni Laterano, Gianicolo, looking like a little hill in a garden, all can be seen clearly. The Vatican garden seems a flower bed, the Vatican a nondescript building, with little courtyards; all is closed and deserted. There is Monte Mario. And down there the Roman countryside, sinister and bare; from here they must have seen the divisions of the Cadorna passing, company after company, canon after canon. Monterotondo, Tivoli, Frascati, Albano and, farther right, in the distance, that thin line glittering, the sea. Rome! Rome! A blessed name one never tires of uttering; there is a secret somewhere in this sound: Rome! It seems to continue echoing in the ear: Rome! Here it all is...."*

Edmondo De Amicis,
"Ricordi di Roma,"
*Ricordi del 1870-1871,*
Florence: Barbera, 1873.

*Left*
Panoramic view with the Altare della Patria (1885-1911) in the background.

*Top*
Sacred area (third-first century B.C.), Largo di Torre Argentina.

*Left, top*
Carabinieri (policemen) on horseback in the Imperial Forums.

*Left, bottom*
Detail of the fountain in front of the National Roman Museum.

*Top*
A park near the Imperial Forums.

*Top*
Carriages in Piazza di Spagna.

*Right*
The Columns of the Temple of Adrian (145 A.D.), today the stock exchange, Piazza di Pietra.

*Pages 62-63*
Trastevere, the steps of Viale Glorioso.

*Right*
Carriages in Piazza di Spagna.

# GENTLE BAROQUE WATERS

"A great silence, broken only by the sound of falling water...Sylvia comes upon a small deserted square, one wall taken over by an enormous baroque fountain, all statues, decorations, the roar of water. Enchanted, Sylvia gazes at the unreal beauty of the scene...."

*From the original screenplay of* La Dolce Vita, *Federico Fellini, published by Cappelli.*

*Left*
Trevi Fountain (1732-1763).

# THE ROMANS? NOTHING WILL SURPRISE THEM.

*"…The Roman's indifference is a pretence, an ancient pretence come back, not presumption. Flaiano in his An Alien in Rome describes it to perfection: the Roman never marvels at anything. Whoever comes to Rome, it makes no difference to him. He has already seen so much, because he has been around so long and knows he is in one of the loveliest places in the world; there is no question about that."*

*From an interview with Monica Vitti, Italian actress.*

*Left*
The Pantheon (first century B.C.).

*Pages 70-71*
The Spanish Steps (1724-1726) and Trinità dei Monti.

# DROPLETS OF GLISTENING LIGHT

"*What filled me with joy that day was something akin to love – but not love – or at least not that love talked about and sought by men, and not even the sense of beauty. It came not from a woman; nor did it come from my thoughts. I will write and you will understand if I say that it was none other than the mere glorification of Light? I was seated in that garden. I could not see the sun but the air shone with indirect light as if the blue sky had turned to liquid and rained down. Yes, truly, there were ripples, engulfing light. On the musk were flecks like droplets. Yes, truly the light seemed to flow along that wide avenue with golden bubbles left on the branch tips amid the streaming rays.*"

*André Gide,*
Les nourritures terrestres,
*Paris: Gallimard, 1942.*

*Left, top*
The bust of Giovanni Maria Lancisi in the Pincio gardens (eighteenth century) with the pine trees of Villa Borghese in the background.

*Left, bottom*
View from Gianicolo Hill. On the right, San Pietro in Montorio (fifteenth century).

*Top*
The Aventine Hill. Santa Sabina (fifth century A.D.) with the dome of St. Peter's in the background.

*Top*
Sheep along the Via Appia Antica (Old Appia Way).

*Right*
The characteristic pavement of the Via Appia Antica.

*"Antiquity does survive in the countryside: fallow, empty, accursed as the desert, with its great stretches of aqueducts and its herds of big-horned cattle. This is truly beautiful, the antique beauty one has imagined."*

Gustave Flaubert, from a letter to Louis Bouilhet, Rome, April 9, 1851, The Letters of 1830-57, London: Faber & Faber, 1979.

## *T*HE TIBER, TAWNY
## AND TREACHEROUS

*"The boatman who ferried me across yesterday to the other side of the Tiber where, beneath the fine leafy trees, the yellow trelliswork of the bathing establishment rises from the tawny water, told me very seriously, 'My dear sir, too many establishments! Too many! Napoli, Livorno, Civitavecchia, Vicarello! Nowadays there are more establishments than bathers. Of course business is bad.'*

*The "Charon," who for two coins carries bodies and souls from one side of the Tiber to the other and vice versa, is a real river dog: thin but strong, with a white woolly beard which does justice to a face burnt by the sun. He sits solemnly at the stern of one of his boats, called Noah's Ark, leaving his post only to proudly collect the price of the brief river journey in his cap. He has two favorite topics of conversation and they never last longer than the crossing: the explanation of the workings of the pulley, which runs on a taut cord between the two river banks keeping the boat secure, and the description of a journey he made in his youth following the Tiber upstream from Ripetta to Stimigliano. [It was] a voyage of squalls, tempests, choppy water, eddies, vortexes, and turmoil. God save us all, to have made it home again."*

Cesare Pascarella,
"Le Campane di Ripetta,"
Prose 1880-1890,
Turin: S.T.E.N., 1920.

*Top*
Ponte Cestio (first century B.C.)
and the Isola Tiberina.

# AT SUNRISE, AT SUNSET: A UNIQUE LIGHT

"Nothing is comparable in beauty to the outline of the Roman horizon, to the gentle slope of the plains, or to the soft, fleeting contours of the mountains confining it. Often in the countryside the valleys take on the form of an arena, a circus, a hippodrome; the flanks of the hills are cut in terraces, as if the mighty hand of the Romans had shifted all that soil. A peculiar haze spread out in the distance fills out the objects masking what might be harsh or brusque in form. The shadows are never heavy and black. There are no masses of rock and scrub so obscure that a little light does not find its way in. A singularly harmonious hue embraces the land, the heavens, the water. Thanks to imperceptible shades of color all the surfaces blend at their edges, making it impossible to ascertain where one ends and the other commences. You must certainly have admired the landscapes of Claude Lorraine with that light seemingly perfect and lovelier than nature? Well, it is the light of Rome! I never tire of seeing Villa Borghese, or the sun setting on the cypresses of Monte Mario or on the pine trees of Villa Pamphili, planted by Le Notre. Often have I gone up the Tiber to Ponte Molle to delight in the great spectacle of the day's end. The peaks of the Sabina mountains then seem made of lapis lazuli and pale gold, their bases and flanks steeped in a haze of violet or scarlet. Sometimes lovely clouds are carried like light chariots on the evening wind with unequalled grace, explaining the apparition of Olympus' inhabitants beneath this mythological sky. Sometimes Ancient Rome seems to have sent westwards all the purple of its consuls and its Caesars, under the feet of the god of the day. This rich decoration does not vanish so quickly as in our climes: when you believe the tones are about to die away all springs to life again in some other part of the horizon, one twilight after another, and the magic of the sunset is prolonged. It is true that at this hour of rest for the countryside the air no longer reverberates with bucolic songs. There are no more shepherds: Dulcia linquimus arva! But the great victims of Clitumnus are still to be seen, white oxen and herds of half-wild mares descending the banks of the Tiber, come to drink its waters. You would think yourself taken back to the time of the old Sabines or the century of the Arcadian Evander, when the Tiber was called Albula and the pious Aeneas sailed up its unknown waters."

Réné F. Chateaubriand
"Lettre à M. de Fontanes sur la campagne romaine"
Antique Edition for J. M. Gautier, Librairie Droz, Genève, Lille: Librairie Giard, 1951.

Left
Paola Fontana (1612), Via Garibaldi.

Pages 80-81
Ponte Vittorio Emanuele II.

Pages 82-83
Detail of a statue (1667-1669),
Ponte Sant'Angelo (second century A.D.).

# ROME, THE HOME OF POETS

"How often have I fantasized on the steps of Piazza di Spagna, up against Keats' house, caught in the rush of steps like a wheel in that of a watermill!

How often have I rode in a carriage around the Colosseum, that vast receptacle of moonlight and dreams, seemingly fueling the city, quenching a thirst for poetry...."

Jean Cocteau,
Foreword to
The Nagel Guide: Italy.

*Left*
Via Condotti as seen from the Spanish Steps of Trinità dei Monti.

# TWILIGHT IN ROME: A ROSE-COLORED HAZE

"The rumble of carriage wheels came up from the Piazza di Spagna and the Pincio. A great many people were strolling under the trees in front of the Villa Medici. Two women seated on a stone bench beside the church were keeping watch over some children playing around the obelisk, which shone rosy red under the sunset, and cast a long slanting, blue-gray shadow. The air freshened as the sun sank lower. Farther off, the city stood out golden against the colorless clear sky, which made the cypresses on Monte Mario look jet black."

Gabriele d'Annunzio,
The Child of Pleasure,
London: William Heinemann, 1898.

*Top*
Via Sistina. In the background, the
Sallust Obelisk (second-third centuries A.D.)

## SOLEMN AND MAJESTIC RISES THE GREAT DOME

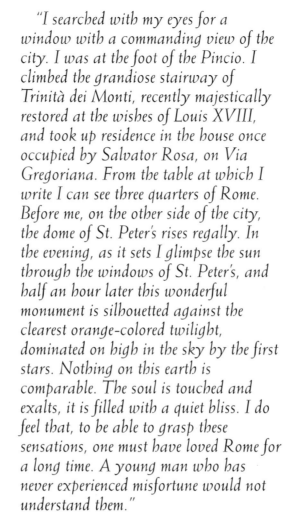

*"I searched with my eyes for a window with a commanding view of the city. I was at the foot of the Pincio. I climbed the grandiose stairway of Trinità dei Monti, recently majestically restored at the wishes of Louis XVIII, and took up residence in the house once occupied by Salvator Rosa, on Via Gregoriana. From the table at which I write I can see three quarters of Rome. Before me, on the other side of the city, the dome of St. Peter's rises regally. In the evening, as it sets I glimpse the sun through the windows of St. Peter's, and half an hour later this wonderful monument is silhouetted against the clearest orange-colored twilight, dominated on high in the sky by the first stars. Nothing on this earth is comparable. The soul is touched and exalts, it is filled with a quiet bliss. I do feel that, to be able to grasp these sensations, one must have loved Rome for a long time. A young man who has never experienced misfortune would not understand them."*

*Stendhal,*
Les Promenades dans Rome,
*Paris: Colmann Lévy
Editeurs, 1926*

*Right*
The dome of St. Peter's.

*Pages 90-91*
The statues of the Dioscuri on
the Campidoglio.

*Pages 92-93*
An unusual view of Constantine's Arch
(fourth century A.D.), with the tower
of Palazzo Senatorio (sixteenth century) on
the left.

*Pages 94-95*
The fountain (eighth century) of Piazza
Santa Maria in Trastevere.

# SECRET ROME: AN EMOTION AT EVERY TURN

*"In Rome the ruins are not dead. They serve a purpose. They are alive. There is no corner, arch, concealed courtyard, that is not home to some activity."*

Jean Cocteau, Foreword to
The Nagel Guide: Italy.

*Left, top*
Craftsmen in Vicolo dei Cappellari.

*Left, bottom*
Craftsmen in Piazza Navona.

*Top*
Craftsmen in Piazza Farnese.

# A ROMAN IS A ROMAN...

*"Rome is popular, but never bourgeois or stupid. Rome seems not to have different social classes. A Roman is a Roman, whether a baker or a Torlonia prince. The Roman aristocracy has nothing to do with that of the rest of the world. Our aristocrats are yokels, they are simpletons. Here all are equal and this makes Rome and the Romans rather unique."*

*From an interview with Monica Vitti.*

Bottom
The market in Campo de' Fiori.

Right
The market in Piazza della Moretta.

Pages 102-103
The Spanish Steps of Trinità dei Monti (1724-1726).

*Left, top*
A barbershop in Via dei Portoghesi.

*Right, top*
An unusual shutter in Via Nazionale.

*Top*
Detail of a doorway in
Via delle Tre Cannelle.

*Left, top*
A window overlooking Via Margutta.

*Right*
The garden of the Galleria Novella Parigini in Via Margutta.

*Page 107*
The Osteria Margutta in Via Margutta.

*Left*
The Fontana della Botte near the Basilica of Santa Maria in Trastevere.

*Right, top*
A fountain at La Sapienza University, in Via degli Staderari.

*Right, bottom*
The fountain in Piazza della Cancelleria.

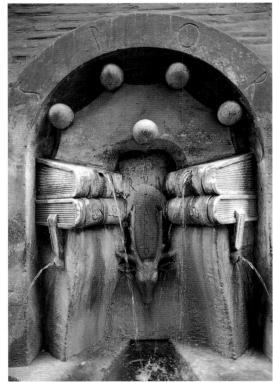

*Top*
The fountain in Via delle Tre Cannelle.

"I often drank in the beauty of Rome, its monuments, its countryside, certain taverns. I used to live at 149 Via Monserrato. Two steps away was the austere and noble Via Giulia, Piazza Farnese with its extraordinary Palazzo, and the long pathetic Tiber. I regret not having painted more often in the open air and not having done more views of Rome. I did in later years. My paintings of those far-off Roman times were if noting else the honest fruit of a sincere need, of a delicate feeling, and sometimes if I see them again it is with some emotion."

*Filippo De Pisis,*
*"La Pittura Romana,"*
Beltempo *magazine.*

*Left*
The arch of Palazzo Farnese (sixteenth century) in Via Giulia.

*Top*
The Campidoglio.

*Right*
The dioscuri.

112

On the inscription: PIVS.VI.PONT.MAX. / QVOD.ABSOLVENDVM.SVPERERAT / ADDITO.CRATERE.EXCITATO.SALIENTE / SYMPLEGMA.CONSVMMAVIT / A.D.MDCCCXVIII.PONTIF.XIX.

On the base: OPVS PHIDIAE

*Top*
Piazza del Quirinale (sixteenth century),
the fountain, the obelisk, and the statues
of Castor and Pollux.

*Right*
Piazza Navona, detail of a statue on the
Fontana dei Fiumi (1650-1651).

# RED HOUSES,
## BAROQUE MELANCHOLY

"It is the liveliest capital in Europe. You have to drive around it in a carriage, steeped in that torrent of carefree ease that denotes the style of a race which keeps its pace to a stroll even when in a hurry. Apart from the areas I have lived in, the Rome I like most is baroque Rome, especially Piazza Navona. I do like Piazza del Quirinale. Those red houses at dusk, those Roman sunsets that induce melancholy, the colors of Scipione and Mafai, somewhat funereal. This is the special charm of Rome."

From an interview with
Vittorio Gasman, Italian actor.

## *Everything comes alive,*
## *all is throbbing*

*"Speak to me stones, talk you towering palaces! Roads, utter a word! Genius, do you move no more? Yes, all is within your sacred walls, eternal Rome, alive; only for me is all mysteriously so. Who shall love me, at which window will I see the gracious creature to me passion and solace? Still no indication of the streets along which continuously to and fro to see her I shall sacrifice precious time? Now I observe churches, palaces, ruins, and columns, as a discerning man who from his journey draws active profit.*

*Yet soon it will end, since one temple alone, the temple of love, shall be the one to welcome the initiate. A world you are in truth, Rome; and yet without love the world would not be the world, nor Rome, Rome."*

Johan Wolfgang Goethe,
*"Elegie romane".*

*Left*
The Fontana delle Tartarughe, or Turtle Fountain, (1581-1588), Piazza Mattei.

*Top*
Fontana del Tritone, or Fountain of the Triton, (1642), Piazza Barberini.

117

# HIDDEN ROME

*"At the corner of the solitary lane,
where no sound is heard but the gurgle of
an invisible fountain, a lamp dimly
illuminates a small Madonna, the odd
silver heart shining out from the bunches
of withered flowers all around her."*

Cesare Pascarella    *"Le Campane di Ripetta,"*
Prose 1880-1890,
*Turin: S.T.E.N.,* 1920.

*Left, top*
A frieze on a house opposite Trevi Fountain.

*Right*
A glimpse of the German Cemetery,
Vatican City.

*Page 119*
Frieze with the Virgin Mary, Palazzo Chigi
(seventeenth century).

# THE ETERNAL ROMAN SPIRIT

*"The number of masterpieces found in
Rome is frightening and overwhelming.
One feels even smaller than in the desert."*

*Gustave Flaubert*

Correspondence
Deuxième Série
(1850-1854),
*Paris : Bibliothèque
Charpentier, 1907.*

*Page 120*
Inside the church of Santa Maria in Aracoeli
(eighth-fourteenth centuries), Campidoglio.

*Page 121*
Inside the church of San Giovanni in
Laterano (fourteenth century).

*Pages 122-123*
Detail of Bernini's colonnade in St. Peter's
(1656-1667).

*Pages 124-125*
The Fontana dei Fiumi (1650-1651),
Piazza Navona.

*Pages 126-127*
Via dei Fori Imperiali (second century B.C.)
with the Torre delle Milizia (eighth century)
behind it to the left.

*Page 128*
The Fontana dei Fiumi, Piazza Navona.